Look and Play
Puppies
by Jim Pipe

Aladdin/Watts
London · Sydney

puppy

A **puppy** is
a baby dog.

3

fur

4

A puppy has **fur**.

5

paws

6

A puppy
has **paws**.

7

eyes

A puppy
has **eyes**.

8

ears

A puppy
has **ears**.

9

nose

A puppy has a **nose**.

10

run

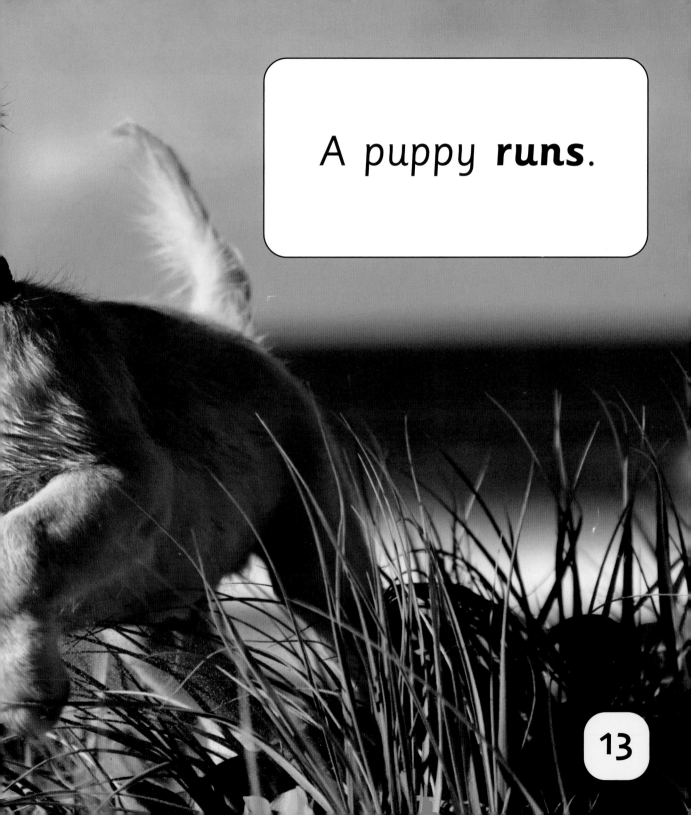

A puppy **runs**.

13

play

14

A puppy **plays**.

15

feed

16

A puppy *feeds*.

17

sleep

18

A puppy **sleeps**.

19

What am I?

paw

eye

ear

nose

Match the words and pictures.

How many?

Can you count the puppies?　**21**

What I need

Walk

Bone

Brush

Bath

How do you care for a puppy?

Index

ear
page 9

eye
page 8

feed
page 16

fur
page 4

nose
page 10

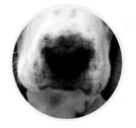

paw
page 6

play
page 14

puppy
page 2

run
page 12

sleep
page 18

For Parents and Teachers

Questions you could ask:

p. 2 What are these puppies doing? The four puppies are drinking their mother's milk. As they grow older, they will begin to eat meat. A group of puppies born at the same time is known as a "litter".

p. 4 What is going on? These puppies are being washed. Like people, their hair needs shampoo! Many puppies also enjoy being rubbed dry.

p. 6 Can you see the claws? Puppies can have sharp claws, but these can be trimmed (like our nails when they get too long).

p. 8 Look at the ears! These Basset Hound puppies have long ears. Compare with other dogs in the book.

p. 10 What sort of dog is this? Dalmatians have black and white spotted coats. Different types or breeds of dog have different features. What different colours can the reader find in the book?

p. 12 Where is the collar? A collar allows a lead to be attached for walks. A collar can also contain information that will help if a dog gets lost.

p. 14 What is this puppy doing? Catching a stick. Puppies love to play. Sticks and puppy toys also give them something to chew on as their teeth grow.

p. 18 Do puppies like to sleep? Yes, like babies, puppies need as much sleep as they can get, often over 14 hours a day.

Activities you could do:

• Use a raw potato cut with a paw shape to make paw prints. These could be placed on the floor to make a "follow the paw" obstacle course.

• Role play: encourage the reader to act out how to look after a puppy (perhaps using a stuffed toy), e.g. feeding, cleaning, walks, giving it a place to sleep.

• Play a game based on "Simon says" where you are a trainer and the readers are puppies obeying your commands. Ask them to do tricks like run, roll over, growl, wag their tail and bark loudly.

• Cut out pictures of different breeds of dog from magazines and compare them, e.g. size, colour.

© Aladdin Books Ltd 2008

Designed and produced by
Aladdin Books Ltd
PO Box 53987
London SW15 2SF

First published in 2008
by Franklin Watts
338 Euston Road
London NW1 3BH

Franklin Watts Australia
Level 17/207 Kent Street
Sydney, NSW 2000

All rights reserved
Printed in Malaysia

A catalogue record for this book is available from the British Library.

Dewey Classification: 636.7

ISBN 978 0 7496 8617 8

Franklin Watts is a division of Hachette Children's Books, an Hachette Livre UK company.
www.hachettelivre.co.uk

Series consultant
Zoe Stillwell is an experienced Early Years teacher currently teaching at Pewley Down Infant School, Guildford.

Photocredits:
l-left, r-right, b-bottom, t-top, c-centre, m-middle. All photos from istockphoto.com except: 2-3, 22bl — Comstock. 14-15, 23tmr – Anke Van Wyk/Dreamstime.com.